Vocabulary Workbook

PEARSON

Scott
Foresman

Editorial Offices: Glenview, Illinois • Parsippany, New Jersey • New York, New York
Sales Offices: Parsippany, New Jersey • Duluth, Georgia • Glenview, Illinois
Coppell, Texas • Ontario, California • Mesa, Arizona

www.sfsocialstudies.com

ISBN 0-328-09064-6

5 6 7 8 9 10 V011 12 11 10 09 08 07 06

© Scott Foresman 1

Name _____

Sounds Like Zoo

Write a word for each picture.

| group | school | rule |

1. _____

2. _____

3. _____

 Directions: Say each word on your vocabulary cards out loud. Pick the three words that have the same sound as the *oo* in *zoo*. Look at the pictures. Write each word on the line next to its correct picture.

Home Activity: Invite your child to make a list of words with the same vowel sound as *school, group,* and *rule.* Have your child group the words according to how /ü/ is spelled.

Name _____

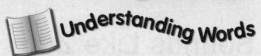Understanding Words

At School

Color two pictures that show things you use in **school**.

| school | flag | rule | group | country |

a.

b.

c.

Draw a picture of a **school**.

 Directions: Look at each picture. *Top:* Color the two pictures that show things that you use in school. *Bottom:* Draw a picture of a school.

 Home Activity: Talk together with your child about some other things used in school and the activities associated with them.

Vocabulary Workbook

Name _____

 Understanding Words

Finding Clues

Draw lines to match.

school	flag	rule	group	country

1. This is our **country**.

a.

2. I follow a **rule**.

b.

3. The **flag** is red, white, and blue.

c.

4. We play in a **group**.

d.

 Directions: Read the sentences, and then match each sentence with a picture at the right. Draw a line from each sentence to its picture.

 Home Activity: Talk together with your child about the meaning of the words *country*, *rule*, *flag*, and *group*.

© Scott Foresman 1

Vocabulary Workbook

Your Day

Narrative Writing

What did you do today? **Write** words to finish the sentences.

| school | flag | rule | group | country |

1. I went to _____.

2. I followed a class _____.

3. I played with a _____.

Write about your day. **Draw** a picture of what you did today.

_____

_____

_____

_____

_____

_____

 Directions: Read the words in the word box.
Top: Write the word that finishes each
sentence on the blank line. *Bottom:* Write a
sentence that describes a part of your day.
Draw a picture about your sentence.

 Home Activity: Together with your child,
create sentences using the vocabulary words.

© Scott Foresman 1

school

group

flag

country

rule

A number of persons or things. I have a <u>group</u> of friends at school.

The place where we learn. I take a bus to <u>school</u>.

A land where a group of people live. My <u>country</u> is the United States of America.

A symbol that stands for a country. The American <u>flag</u> is a symbol of our country.

Something that tells us what to do and what not to do. One <u>rule</u> we have at school is to only cross the street with the crossing guard.

Clapping Game

Write the number of parts of each word.

| neighborhood | law | state | ocean |
| community | leader | continent | |

1. neighborhood _____

2. law _____

3. state _____

4. ocean _____

5. community _____

6. leader _____

7. continent _____

Which word has the most parts? _____

 Directions: *Top:* Read the words in the box out loud with me. Clap once for each part of the word that you hear. Write the number of parts you hear on the line next to each word. *Bottom:* Write the word that has the most parts on the line.

 Home Activity: Invite your child to play a clapping game to show how many parts there are in different words.

What Do You Do?

What does each person do? **Write** the new word on the line.
Draw a picture of that person.

1. lead + [er] =

   leader

3. teach + [er] =

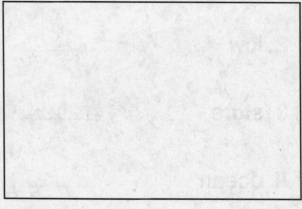

2. farm + [er] =

4. read + [er] =

© Scott Foresman 1

Community Picture

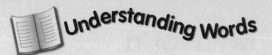
Understanding Words

What makes a **community**? On each line **write** the part of the **community** that the arrow points to.

(school)   (street)   (park)   (house)

A Community

Directions: Look at the picture of a community. Look at the thing each arrow points to. Choose a word from the circles. Write the name of each thing on the line.

Home Activity: Discuss other parts of your own community with your child. Have your child make drawings of those other parts of a community. Remember, people are part of a community, too.

© Scott Foresman 1

Name _____

My World

Narrative Writing

Write one word to finish each sentence.

| neighborhood | law | state | ocean |
| community | leader | continent | |

1. Florida is a _____.

2. North America is a _____.

3. Fish swim in the _____.

Write about where you live.
Draw a picture to show where you live.

_____

_____

_____

_____

_____

 Directions: Read the words in the word box.
Top: Write the words that finish each
sentence. *Bottom:* Write to describe where
you live. Draw a picture about your sentence.

 Home Activity: Invite your child to read what
he or she wrote. Talk about some other ways
you could describe your neighborhood or the
larger world around you.

neighborhood

community

law

leader

A group of people and the place where they live. I live in a big <u>community</u> with many neighborhoods.

A place where people live, work, and play. I like the <u>neighborhood</u> where I live.

Someone who helps people decide what to do. The <u>leader</u> of a community is called a mayor.

A rule that people must obey. It is a <u>law</u> that cars must stop at stop signs.

state

continent

ocean

A very large piece of
land. South America
is a <u>continent</u>.

A part of a country.
Florida is a <u>state</u> in
our country.

A very large body of salt
water. An <u>ocean</u> can have
many waves.

ABC Order

How do we put <u>j</u>ump, <u>d</u>irt, and <u>p</u>ot in ABC order?

a b c (d) e f g h i (j) k l m

n o (p) q r s t u v w x y z

<u>d</u>irt   <u>j</u>ump   <u>p</u>ot

Put the words in the word box in ABC order. **Write** one word on each line.

job	wants	goods	volunteer
needs	tools	service	

_____

_____

_____

_____

_____

_____

 Directions: Read the words. To put the words in ABC order, find the first letter of each word by looking at the alphabet. The ABC order of the words is *dirt, jump, pot.* Now put the words in the word box in ABC order. Write one word on each line.

 Home Activity: Work with your child to put things in alphabetical order, such as names, toys, or books.

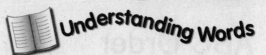
More Than One

Words that mean more than one may end with the letter s.

one pencil	two pencils

Circle the words that mean more than one.

1. (goods)   good

2. tool   tools

3. rulers   ruler

4. cups   cup

5. pen   pens

6. dog   dogs

7. bees   bee

8. grape   grapes

9. boy   boys

10. forks   fork

 Directions: Words that mean more than one may end with s. Read the example: one pencil, two pencils. Circle the word in each pair that means more than one.

 Home Activity: Play this game with your child for plural nouns that are made by adding s. Start by saying "I have one book." Then hold up two fingers. Your child answers "I have two books." Continue by using different nouns and numbers.

Vocabulary Workbook

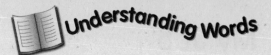

Needs and Wants

Circle **need** or **want** for each picture.

1.

need   (want)

2.

need   want

3.

need   want

4.

need   want

5.

need   want

6.

need   want

 Directions: Look at each picture. Think about needs and wants. Circle **need** if you must have the item to live. Circle **want** if you might like to have the item, but do not need it to live.

 Home Activity: With your child, look through newspapers and magazines for pictures of advertised items. Help your child identify which items are needs and which items are wants.

My Job

Narrative Writing

Write one word to finish each sentence.

job	wants	goods	volunteer
needs	tools	service	transportation

1. A doctor provides a _____ that helps others.

2. A tailor makes _____ that people wear.

3. A plumber uses _____ that help fix leaks.

Write about a job you would like.
Draw a picture of that job.

_____

_____

_____

_____

Directions: Read the words in the word box. *Top:* Write the word from the word box that completes each sentence. *Bottom:* Write a sentence about a job that you would like to have. Draw a picture about your sentence.

Home Activity: Talk with your child about the job he or she wrote about. Help your child to use this unit's vocabulary words to describe the job.

© Scott Foresman 1

job

needs

wants

tools

Things people must have to live. Food is one of our <u>needs</u>.

The work people do. My neighbor's <u>job</u> is to paint houses.

Things that are used to help people do work. Scissors, a ruler, and a pencil are different kinds of <u>tools</u>.

Things we would like to have. Some of my <u>wants</u> are presents and cake.

Name _____

goods

service

volunteer

transportation

© Scott Foresman 1

A job a person does to help others. As a firefighter, my mom provides a <u>service</u> to our neighborhood.

Things that are grown or made. A farmer grows <u>goods</u> such as fruit and vegetables.

A car, bus, or other way that people and goods move from place to place. A school bus is a kind of <u>transportation</u> that takes me to school.

A person who works for free. The <u>volunteer</u> helps children cross the street.

Letter Pairs

Write the words that have the letter pair.

weather	mountain	natural resource
plain	river	

1. **er** _____

_____

2. **ai** _____

_____

Write the word that makes the same **ai** sound as **tr_ai_n**.

_____

3. **ou** _____

_____

Write the word that makes the same **ou** sound as **p_ou_r**.

_____

 Directions: *Number 1:* Write two words from the word box that have the same letter pair. *Number 2:* Write two words from the word box that have the same letter pair. Now say the words with me. Which word makes the same *ai* sound as *train? Number 3:* Write two words from the word box that have the same letter pair. Now say the words with me. Which word makes the same *ou* sound as *pour?*

 Home Activity: Look together with your child at books or magazines you have at home. Invite your child to write down other words with these letter combinations: *ai, er,* and *ou.* Have your child say aloud each word he or she finds. Ask your child to group the words according to the sound each letter pair makes.

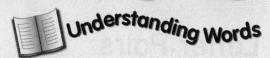

Sound Alikes

Sometimes two words sound the same, but they are not spelled the same and they do not mean the same thing.

The **weather** will be sunny.
I do not know **whether** I can go or not.

Draw lines to match.

 pair  plane

 male see

 sea pear

 plain  mail

 Directions: Read with me. "Sometimes two words sound the same, but they are not spelled the same and they do not mean the same thing." Read the example: "The weather will be sunny. I do not know whether I can go or not." What words sound the same in the two sentences? Look at each picture and read its name out loud. Draw lines to match each word with the word that sounds the same.

Home Activity: Challenge your child to use each homophone in a sentence.

Land and Water

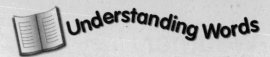
Understanding Words

Write the word that describes the picture. **Color** to show if it is land or water.

river	mountain	plain	lake

1.

_____

2.

_____

3.

_____

4.

_____

Directions: Look at each picture. Write the word on the line that describes the picture. If the picture is of land, color it green or brown. If the picture is of water, color it blue.

Home Activity: Look together with your child for pictures of lakes, rivers, plains, or mountains in books or magazines.

Weather

Narrative Writing

People do different things in different weather. Think about your favorite kind of weather. **Write** to explain your favorite weather. Describe what things you do in your favorite weather. Use vocabulary words if possible. You may use another sheet of paper if needed.

plain	river	mountain	lake

_____

_____

_____

_____

_____

_____

_____

_____

 Directions: Follow along as I read. People do different things in different weather. Think about your favorite kind of weather. **Write** to explain your favorite weather. Describe what things you do in your favorite weather. Use vocabulary words if possible. You may use another sheet of paper if needed.

 Home Activity: Look at a weather forecast with your child on television, on the Internet, or in your local newspaper. Together, discuss what types of activities you might be able to do each day based on the weather.

© Scott Foresman 1

weather

mountain

plain

lake

The highest kind of land. The <u>mountain</u> has snow on the top.

How it is outside at a certain place and time. The <u>weather</u> is stormy with lightning.

A large body of water that has land either totally or almost totally around it. A <u>lake</u> is smaller than an ocean.

A large, mostly flat piece of land. This farm is on a <u>plain</u>.

river

natural
resource

history

A useful thing that comes from nature. Water is a <u>natural resource</u>.

A long body of water which usually moves toward a lake or the ocean. We traveled down the <u>river</u> in a boat.

The story of people and places from the past. I like reading about what people in our country's <u>history</u> wore.

Vocabulary Workbook

Name _____

Give Me a Hint

Draw a ☼ for words about the day. **Draw** a ☾ for words about the night.

┌─────────────────┐
│   │
│   │
│   │
└─────────────────┘
        daytime

┌─────────────────┐
│   │
│   │
│   │
└─────────────────┘
        midnight

┌─────────────────┐
│   │
│   │
│   │
└─────────────────┘
       nightmare

┌─────────────────┐
│   │
│   │
│   │
└─────────────────┘
       nightgown

┌─────────────────┐
│   │
│   │
│   │
└─────────────────┘
        daylight

┌─────────────────┐
│   │
│   │
│   │
└─────────────────┘
       daydream

Write other words you know with **day** in them.

_____

_____

Direction: Look at the word *holiday* on the board. A holiday is a special day. The word *day* in *holiday* gives you a hint about what *holiday* means. *Top:* Draw a sun for words about the day. Draw a crescent moon for words about the night. *Bottom:* Think about other words you know that have the word *day* in them. Write them on the lines.

Home Activity: Challenge your child to make a list of other words with the word part *day*. Help your child make another list for the word part *free*.

Common and Proper

Common Noun	Proper Noun
month	April
state	Florida
boy	John

Draw lines to match the nouns.

1. holiday

Washington, D.C.

2. colony

Veterans Day

3. capital

Virginia

 Directions: Common nouns name any person, place, or thing. Proper nouns name a special person, place, or thing. Proper nouns begin with a capital letter. Read the common and proper nouns: *month/April, state/Florida, boy/John.* Look at the pictures. Draw a line from each common noun to the proper noun example.

 Home Activity: Invite your child to identify nouns in a storybook. Challenge your child to give a common noun counterpart for each proper noun.

Name _____

Using Picture Clues

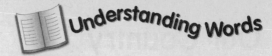 Understanding Words

freedom	holiday	citizen	colony
President	vote	capital	

1. Circle the picture that shows a **holiday** celebrating **freedom**.

2. Circle the picture that shows how people **vote**.

3. Circle the picture that shows something you would find in our country's **capital**.

 Directions: Look at the pictures. For *1*, circle the picture that shows a holiday that celebrates freedom. For *2*, circle the picture that shows how a person votes. For *3*, circle the picture that shows something you would find in our country's capital.

 Home Activity: Talk with your child about the meanings of the words in the word box. Ask your child to draw pictures to illustrate something that reflects the meaning of these words.

Name _____

Our Country

Expository Writing

We Americans are proud of our history and our people. Think about what you have learned about your country. **Write** to explain something about your country that makes you proud. Use vocabulary words. You may use another sheet of paper if needed.

freedom	**holiday**	**citizen**	**capital**	**colony**
President	**vote**			

_____

_____

_____

_____

_____

_____

Directions: Follow along as I read. We Americans are proud of our history and our people. Think about what you have learned about your country. **Write** to explain something about your country that makes you proud. Use vocabulary words. You may use another sheet of paper if needed.

Home Activity: Talk with your child about the ways in which Americans show pride. Look through newspapers and magazines to find pictures that show Americans showing pride.

Vocabulary Workbook

freedom

colony

holiday

President

A place that is ruled by a country that is far away. Virginia was once a <u>colony</u>.

A person's right to make choices. Many people in the United States show flags to celebrate their <u>freedom</u>.

Our country's leader. The <u>President</u> of the United States makes many important decisions.

A special day. Independence Day is a <u>holiday</u>.

citizen

vote

capital

✂

A choice that gets counted. Citizens of the United States <u>vote</u> for a new President every four years.

A member of a state and country. I am a <u>citizen</u> of the United States of America.

The city where important leaders of a state or country live and work. Washington, D.C. is the <u>capital</u> of the United States.

Name _____

Related Words

Draw lines to match words that are related.

1. play   **a.** marketplace

2. invention   **b.** world

3. communication   **c.** graph

4. market   **d.** inventor

5. printer   **e.** information

6. inform   **f.** playful

7. graphic   **g.** print

8. worldwide   **h.** communicate

 Directions: Draw lines to match words that are related. Look at the example. *Play* is related to *playful*. The word *play* is a part of both words. Someone who is playful likes to play.

 Home Activity: Invite your child to describe how the related words are related. For instance, a printer is someone who prints something.

Name _____

Who Am I?

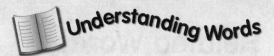
Understanding Words

Write the word on the line to make a new word.

1. I <u>invent</u> things.

I am an ___invent__ | or | .

3. I <u>sail</u> on the sea.

I am a _____ | or | .

2. I <u>act</u> on stage.

I am an _____ | or | .

4. I <u>direct</u> movies.

I am a _____ | or | .

Directions: Look at each picture. What do you call each person? Rewrite the underlined word to make a new word that ends with *-or*.

Home Activity: Invite your child to make a list of other "one who" words that end with *-or* and to describe what each person does.

© Scott Foresman 1

Name _____

Communicating

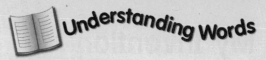

Understanding Words

Color the picture of each **invention** that helps you **communicate**.

1.

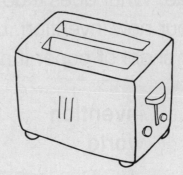

2. Describe the ways that you **communicate**.

_____

_____

_____

 Directions: *Top:* Look at the pictures. Which inventions are used to communicate thoughts and ideas? Color the picture of each invention that is used to communicate. *Bottom:* Write about the ways that you communicate.

Home Activity: Challenge your child to talk about different ways your family communicates with one another and with other relatives.

My Invention

Narrative Writing

People invent new things every day. Think of an invention that you would like to make. What does it do? How does it work? **Write** to describe your new invention. Use vocabulary words. You may use another sheet of paper if needed.

market	**invention**	**communicate**
inventor	**world**	

_____

_____

_____

_____

_____

_____

_____

_____

 Directions: Follow along as I read. People invent new things every day. Think of an invention that you would like to make. What does it do? How does it work? **Write** to describe your new invention. Use vocabulary words. You may use another sheet of paper if needed.

 Home Activity: Invite your child to read aloud his or her writing. Show your child things that have been invented during your lifetime, such as a microwave oven or CD player. Describe how things were different before these inventions.

© Scott Foresman 1

market

communicate

invention

inventor

world

Give and get information. People can use a telephone to <u>communicate</u>.

A place where goods are sold. We buy fruit at the <u>market</u>.

Someone who makes or invents something new. Alexander Graham Bell was a famous <u>inventor</u>.

Something new. The telephone was an important <u>invention</u>.

A name for Earth and everything on it. The picture shows how the <u>world</u> looks from space.